Katherine Johnson

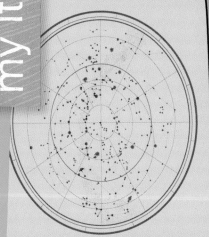

Published in the United States of America by Cherry Lake Publishing
Ann Arbor, Michigan
www.cherrylakepublishing.com

Content Adviser: Ryan Emery Hughes, Doctoral Student, School of Education, University of Michigan
Reading Adviser: Marla Conn MS, Ed., Literacy specialist, Read-Ability, Inc.
Book Design: Jennifer Wahi
Illustrator: Jeff Bane

Photo Credits: © Mark Ross/Shutterstock, 5; © Dr Project/Shutterstock, 7; © Atstock Productions/ Shutterstock, 9; © Aspen Photo/Shutterstock, 11; © NASA, 13, 22; © NASA, 15; © NASA Langley Research Center, 17; © NASA, 19, 23; © (NASA/Aubrey Gemignani), 21; Cover, 12, 16, 18, Jeff Bane; Various frames throughout, © Shutterstock Images

Library of Congress Cataloging-in-Publication Data

Names: Loh-Hagan, Virginia, author. | Bane, Jeff, 1957- illustrator.
Title: Katherine Johnson / by Virginia Loh-Hagan ; [illustrator, Jeff Bane].
Other titles: My itty-bitty bio.
Description: Ann Arbor, MI : Cherry Lake Publishing, [2018] | Series: My itty-bitty bio | Audience: K to grade 3. | Includes index.
Identifiers: LCCN 2017029646| ISBN 9781534107106 (hardcover) | ISBN 9781534108097 (pbk.) | ISBN 9781534109087 (pdf) | ISBN 9781534120075 (hosted ebook)
Subjects: LCSH: Johnson, Katherine, 1918---Juvenile literature. | United States. National Aeronautics and Space Administration--Biography--Juvenile literature. | African American women mathematicians--Biography--Juvenile literature. | African American women physicists--Biography--Juvenile literature. | Women mathematicians--Biography--Juvenile literature. | Women physicists--Biography--Juvenile literature. | African American women--Juvenile literature.
Classification: LCC QA29.J64 L64 2018 | DDC 510.92 [B] --dc23
LC record available at https://lccn.loc.gov/2017029646

Printed in he United States of America
Corporate Graphics

About the author: Dr. Virginia Loh-Hagan is an author, university professor, former classroom teacher, and curriculum designer. Like Katherine, she speaks her mind. Her husband has a degree in math. She lives in San Diego with her very tall husband and very naughty dogs. To learn more about her, visit: www.virginialoh.com

About the illustrator: Jeff Bane and his two business partners own a studio along the American River in Folsom, California, home of the 1849 Gold Rush. When Jeff's not sketching or illustrating for clients, he's either swimming or kayaking in the river to relax.

I was born in West Virginia.
It was 1918.

I counted everything. I loved math. I was smart.

$-P_r(1-\cos\varphi)$; $\quad \dfrac{P_r^3}{EJ}\dfrac{(1-\cos\alpha)^2}{2}$;

$P\cos\varphi$

$\dfrac{P_r^3}{EJ}\left(\dfrac{3}{2}a - 2\sin\alpha + \dfrac{\sin 2\alpha}{4}\right)$;

$M_1 = -\dfrac{qx_1^2}{2}$; $\quad \overline{M}_1 = -1\cdot x_1$;

$\dfrac{P_r^2}{EJ}\left(\alpha - \sin a\right)$;

$P\sin\varphi$

$\lambda = \dfrac{EJ}{GJ_k}$; $\quad \dfrac{mr}{EJ}\dfrac{\lambda-1}{2}\sin^2 a$;

$\dfrac{m}{EJ}\left(\dfrac{1+\lambda}{2}a - \dfrac{\lambda-1}{4}\sin 2a\right)$;

What do you like to count?

Some schools didn't want me.
They didn't respect blacks.

They didn't respect women.

I finished college. I was 18.
I went to **graduate** school.

I was one of three black
students. I was the only woman.

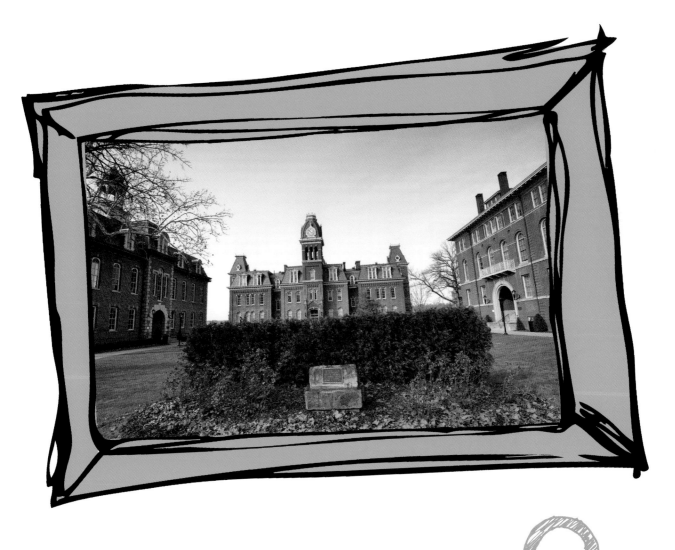

What do you want to learn?

NASA hired me. I was a "human **computer**." I did math.

Women and blacks were treated unfairly. Women couldn't put their names on their work.

I changed this.

Have you ever been treated unfairly?

Only men went to meetings.
I didn't care. I went.

I asked questions. I shared
ideas.

I figured out flight **paths**.
I helped **spacecraft** go
around Earth.

I was important. I helped our future.

My math sent people to the moon and back!

What would you like to ask me?

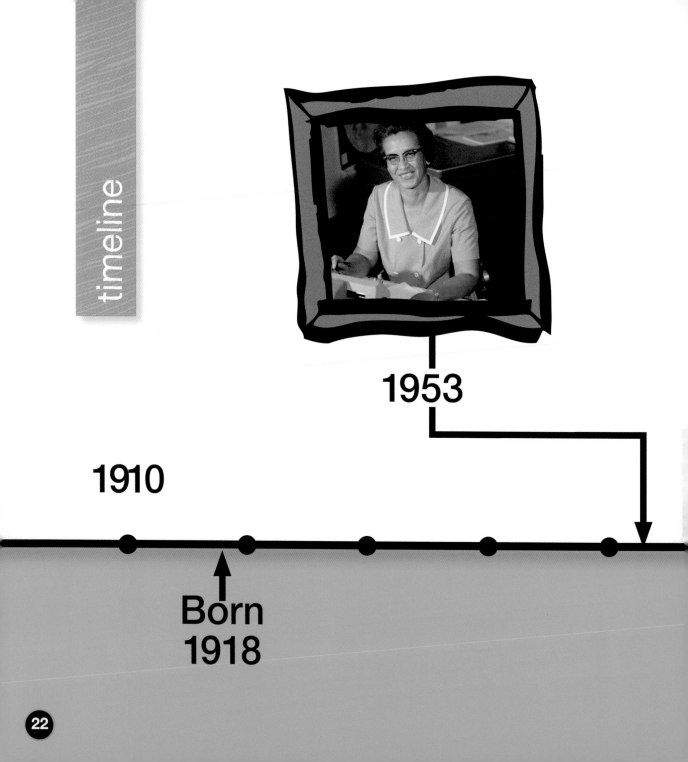

1953

1910

Born
1918

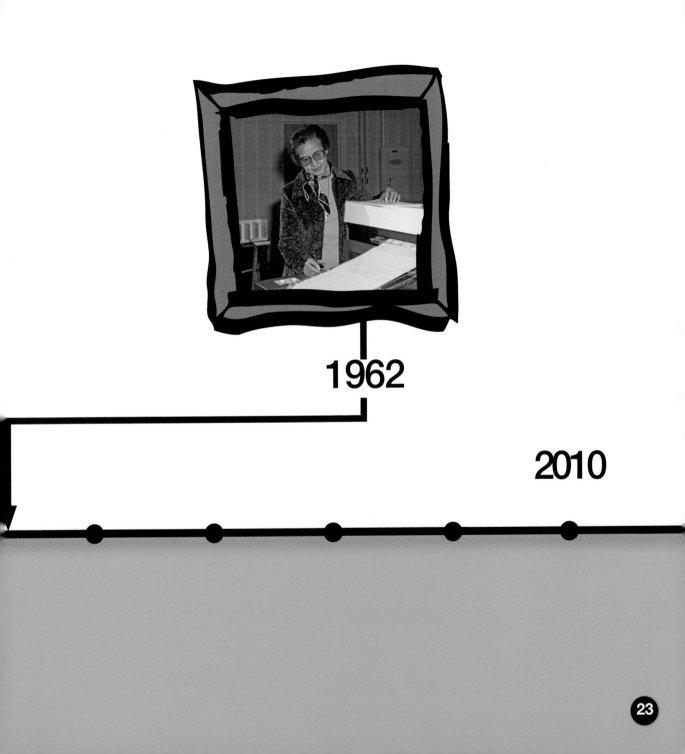

1962

2010

glossary

computer (kuhm-PYOO-tur) a machine that can do really hard math problems; a person who can do this is called a "human computer"

graduate (GRAJ-oo-it) schooling that comes after college, like master's or doctorate programs

NASA (NASS-uh) the National Aeronautics and Space Administration; it is in charge of the United States' space program

paths (PATHS) the ways something will travel to and in space

spacecraft (SPAYS-kraft) machines that go to space, like shuttles and rockets

index